LAZY LUCK

Get Money, Love
and Happiness
→ with ←
Feng Shui
(*The Super Easy Way*)

LINDA RUBRIGHT

Lazy Luck: Get Money, Love and Happiness with Feng Shui (The Super Easy Way) by Linda Rubright

Copyright © 2020 by Linda Rubright

All rights reserved. No part of this book may be reproduced, distributed or transmitted in any form or by any means, including photocopying, recording or other electronic or mechanical methods, without the prior written permission of the publisher, except in the case of brief quotations embodied in critical reviews. For permission requests, write to the author at linda@happyhousefengshui.com.

Limit of Liability / Disclaimer of Warranty
The author has used her best efforts in preparing this book. The author makes no representations or warranties with respect to the accuracy or completeness of the contents of this book and specifically disclaim any implied warranties with respect to the accuracy or completeness of the book and specifically disclaim any implied warranties and merchantability or fitness for a particular purpose. There are no warranties which extend beyond the descriptions contained in the paragraph. The author shall not be liable for any loss of profit or any other commercial damages, including but not limited to special, incidental, consequential or other damages.

Special discounts are available on quantity purchases. For details, contact the author at linda@happyhousefengshui.com.

Printed in these fabulous United States of America

If you could...

Move a few things around in your house and get more love, luck, money and happiness - why on earth wouldn't you?

The practice of doing this is called Feng Shui.

Doing Feng Shui super easily is what this book is all about.

Table of Contents

Getting Started
What's Feng Shui?..8
The Two Ways to Do Feng Shui..9
The Only Question You Need to Ask About
Decluttering...12

Feng Shui By Room Type
How to Do Feng Shui By Room Type....................................14
Bedroom: For Love and Restful Sleep..................................15
Living Room: For Your Social Life/Entertainment 17
Kitchen: For Your Health..18
Bathroom: For Wellness and Vitality 20
Dining Room: For Holding onto Health & Wealth..................21
Office/Cube: For Success 22
Front Door: For Career and Overall Energy of your Home..24
Yard: or the Energy that Surrounds You..............................25
Closets, Drawers, Garage, Storage: For What
You (Emotionally, Psychologically, Physically, etc.)
Hold On To 27

Feng Shui by Goal in Any Room
How to Do Feng Shui by Goal in Any Room.........................29
Where Each Feng Shui Life Area is in a Room....................30
Money...31
Fame & Reputation...32

Table of Contents (cont.)

Feng Shui by Goal in Any Room(cont.)
Love & Marriage...33
Family..35
Health...37
Creativity & Children...38
Wisdom & Knowledge...39
Career..40
Helpful People & Travel 41

The "Why" Behind What You Add, Remove and Change
Bedroom..44
Living Room..48
Kitchen..50
Bathroom..53
Dining Room...55
Office/Cube..58
Front Door..61
Yard...64
Closets, Drawers, Garage & Storage............................66
Money...69
Fame & Reputation...72
Love & Marriage..75
Family...78
Health...80
Creativity & Children..82
Wisdom & Knowledge..84
Career..86
Helpful People & Travel..89

Table of Contents (cont.)

FAQs and Examples of Room Layouts
FAQs..92
Examples of Different Room Layouts..98

Tips
Pregnancy & Fertility..16
Losing Weight..19
Improve Work Relationships..23
Improve Relationships with Neighbors..26
Love & Marriage Tips..34
Improve Family Relationships..36
How to Make Your Wishes Come True..42

Contact Me..100

Getting Started

What's Feng Shui?

What happens in your house is what happens in your life. If you can change what's happening in your house - you can change what's happening in your life and Feng Shui shows you how to do just that!

The Two Ways to Do Feng Shui

Start with whichever way sounds easiest or most fun, and do as much - or as little - as feels right with either (or both). Note: There's some overlap in the areas of your life where both methods can assist (e.g. both can help with love). Likewise, there's some uniqueness in each approach (e.g., the first approach can help with rest and the second can help with travel). If you want to work on areas where there's overlap, start with the method that feels the best, and then do as much as you can as long as it feels right and fun.

The First Way (The Super Easiest)

In Feng Shui, each room in your house symbolizes a particular goal you might have, such as a better love life (your bedroom) or better health (your kitchen).

Using the following list, decide which room you want to start with. Then, go to that room's page in the book and add or remove as many of the listed items as possible.

- Bedroom: For Restful Sleep and Passion
- Living Room: For Enjoyment and Your Social Life
- Kitchen: For Health

- Bathroom: For Vitality
- Dining Room: For Holding onto Love, Health and Wealth
- Front Door: For Your Career and the Overall Energy of Your Home
- Yard: For The Energy that Surrounds You
- Office / Cube: For Your Success and Empowerment
- Closets & Drawers: For What You Hold On To

The Second Way (Also Incredibly Easy)

Every room in your home can be divided into nine parts. Each individual part is symbolic of the nine different goals you may have where Feng Shui can help:

- Money
- Fame & Your Reputation
- Love & Marriage
- Family (Friends & Community)
- Health
- Creativity & Children
- Skills & Knowledge
- Career
- Helpful People & Travel

Determine which area of your life you'd like to start with and go to that area's page in the book. Then, go to the room you use most often and follow the easy instructions on how to locate that particular area in the room. Then, add or remove as many of the listed items as possible.

If helpful, see examples of different room layouts on pages 98 and 99.

The Only Question You Need to Ask about Decluttering

Start with a room, a corner of a room, or even a drawer—whatever feels least overwhelming—and look at each item in that space. Ask yourself:

"Do I love this dearly or use this yearly?"

If the answer is yes, keep it. If the answer is no, donate, recycle, or toss it. Then, move on to the next least overwhelming room, corner, or drawer, – and so on. In other words, absolutely keep the things you deeply love, but also keep the things that are necessary to make your life work every year. (Assuming, of course, you use them every year.) And if anything doesn't fit into one or both of those categories, get rid of it in the most environmentally-friendly way possible, please.

How to Do Feng Shui by Room Type

How to Do Feng Shui by Room

Step One
Choose the room whose symbolic meaning you most want help with (see below), the room you use the most or the room you think needs the most improvement.

- Bedroom: Restful Sleep and Passion
- Living Room: Enjoyment and Your Social Life
- Kitchen: Health
- Bathroom: Vitality
- Dining Room: Holding onto Health and Wealth
- Office / Cube: Success and Empowerment
- Front Door: Career and the Overall Energy of Your Home
- Yard: The Energy that Surrounds You
- Closets & Drawers: What You Hold On To

Step Two
Go to that room's page in the book and add, remove or improve as many of the items as possible in the respective room. Then, move onto the next room, as desired.

Bedroom

Represents Restful Sleep and Passion
Allow it to be a Sanctuary for Rest and Love

Add, remove or improve as many of the following items as possible in your bedroom.

+

- ○ Solid headboard
- ○ Wall at the head of the bed
- ○ Identical nightstands and lamps
- ○ Comfortable mattress and sheets
- ○ Ability to see the door while you lay in bed
- ○ Art/symbols of love and intimacy
- ○ Ability to easily approach the bed from either side
- ○ Dimmer on lights
- ○ Symbols of the person you'd like to meet or photos of you and your partner
- ○ Red and/or pink accents
- ○ Candles and good scents
- ○ Any identical objects in pairs of two
- ○ Close bedroom and closet doors and drawers at night

−

- ○ Using someone else's mattress
- ○ Electronics, TVs, computers, books, paperwork, bills, work or fitness equipment
- ○ Photos/symbols of anyone (including religious figures) except you and your partner
- ○ Dirty laundry
- ○ Twin bed
- ○ Too much white
- ○ Mirror facing the bed
- ○ Storage under the bed or anything hanging above your head
- ○ Water or symbols of it
- ○ Bed up against a window
- ○ Reminders of old relationships, bad times or anything negative
- ○ Reminders of why it's hard to sleep
- ○ Clutter, dirt, dust, messes, dead plants

Pregnancy & Fertility Tips!

- In your bedroom, put the identical number of objects that match your ideal number of family members.

- Remove anything from the bedroom that reminds you of the reasons it's hard to get pregnant.

- Pay special attention to your Health area, Family area and Creativity & Children area.

Living Room

Represents Enjoyment and Your Social Life
Allow it to be Comfortable, Welcoming and Fun

Add, remove or improve as many of the following items as possible in your living room.

+

- ○ Sofa against a wall
- ○ Place the sofa so you can clearly see the main entrance while seated
- ○ Open windows, curtains and blinds regularly
- ○ Symbols, objects and reminders of the things you want to do and want to do more of
- ○ Photos of happy times and people you enjoy

−

- ○ Furniture against a window
- ○ Anything reminders of bad times
- ○ Anything that reminds you of people you don't want to spend time with
- ○ Dead plants
- ○ Clutter, dirt, dust, messes

Kitchen

Represents Health
Allow it to be Vibrant and in Excellent Condition

Add, remove or improve as many of the following items as possible in the kitchen.

+

- ○ Immaculate stove and oven
- ○ Only keep things on the counter you use daily
- ○ Symbols and reminders of what health looks like to you
- ○ Good lighting
- ○ Yellow
- ○ Bowl of fruit on your table
- ○ Round-leaf plants

−

- ○ Visible knives
- ○ Leaky faucets
- ○ Dirty dishes
- ○ Chipped or broken dishes
- ○ Broken appliances
- ○ Unused or significantly damaged pots/pans
- ○ Anything on the countertops not used daily
- ○ Anything that feels unhappy and unhealthy
- ○ Food 12+ months old that you'll never eat
- ○ Dead plants
- ○ Clutter, dirt, dust, messes

Weight Loss Tips!

- If the kitchen is the first room you see when you enter the house, add a tall plant, rug, piece of art or furniture to distract your attention from it.

- Don't eat off of red, yellow, purple or pink dishes.

- Place photos of you when you were at your desired weight in your kitchen.

- Put symbols of what you'll do or how you'll feel at your desired weight in your kitchen.

- Don't call attention to your refrigerator. Remove anything hung on it.

- If possible, dispose of any objects or memories that make you feel weighed down. Remove these items from the kitchen and any other rooms in the house!

- Pay special attention to the Health area in the rooms of your home.

Bathroom

Represents Vitality
Allow it to be Purifying and Refreshing

Add, remove or improve as many of the following items as possible in your bathroom.

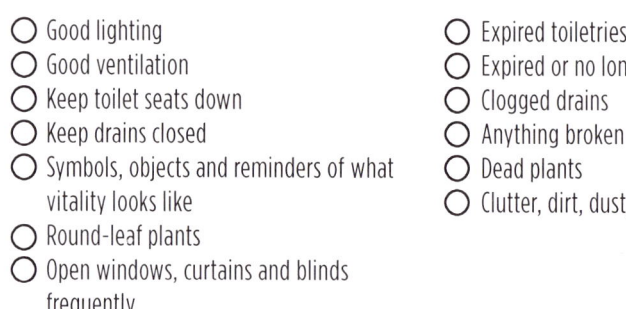

- ○ Good lighting
- ○ Good ventilation
- ○ Keep toilet seats down
- ○ Keep drains closed
- ○ Symbols, objects and reminders of what vitality looks like
- ○ Round-leaf plants
- ○ Open windows, curtains and blinds frequently
- ○ Photos or symbols of nature

- ○ Expired toiletries
- ○ Expired or no longer used medicine
- ○ Clogged drains
- ○ Anything broken or torn
- ○ Dead plants
- ○ Clutter, dirt, dust, messes

Dining Room

Represents Your Ability to Hold onto Love, Health & Wealth
Allow it to Feel Abundant

Add, remove or improve as many of the following items as possible in your dining room.

+

- ○ Table that fits comfortably in the room
- ○ Oval or round table
- ○ Even number of chairs
- ○ Bowl of fruit in the middle of the table
- ○ Round leafed plants near the table
- ○ Reminders of happiness and abundance
- ○ Dimmer on lights
- ○ Photos / symbols of wealth and health
- ○ Mirror that reflects what's on the table
- ○ If your have an open floor plan, use a visual break to delineate the dining room
- ○ Open windows, curtains and blinds regularly

−

- ○ Clocks
- ○ Electronics, TVs, computers
- ○ Chipped or broken dishes
- ○ Seats against windows or with backs to the door
- ○ Glass dining tables
- ○ Dead plants
- ○ Clutter, dirt, dust, messes

Office / Cube
Represents Success and Empowerment
Allow it to be Strong and Inspiring

Add, remove or improve as many of the following items as possible in your office.

+

- Arrange your desk so your back is against a wall (if this isn't possible, put a mirror up so you can see behind you)
- Arrange your desk so you can clearly see the door while seated
- Inspirational images or symbols
- Reminders of where you want your career to go and what your success will look like
- Round-leaf plants
- Successful feeling furniture and decor
- Jade plants
- Any positive stress reliever
- Inspirational quotes

−

- Tangled cords
- Files on your computer you no longer need
- Paperwork you no longer need or use
- Symbols, objects or reminders related to a career you don't want
- Reminders of hard or bad times
- Dead plants
- Clutter, dirt, dust, messes

Tips to Improve Strained Work Relationships!

- Add a glass sphere (e.g., snow globe) in the center of your office to help work go smoothly.

- Hang a picture of you and the troubling co-worker in your office. Note: Nothing in Feng Shui has to be out in the open or visible. Feel free to hide these items behind a piece of furniture, art or in a drawer.

- If you and the troubling co-worker's desks face each other (even if you're on opposite sides of the building), reposition your desk so you're not facing the person. Ideally, you'd have your back to them.

Front Door

Represents Your Career and the Quality
of Energy Entering Your Home
Allow it to Feel Happy and Positive

At and near the door the architect of your home would consider the main entrance, add, remove and/or improve as many of the following items below as possible.

+ **−**

- ○ A clean and very welcoming welcome mat
- ○ Fountain, water or symbols/images of water
- ○ Healthy plants or flowers
- ○ Symbols of the career you want or want to keep
- ○ Wreath and/or welcoming decor
- ○ Wind chimes (as long as they don't annoy the neighbors)
- ○ Mirrors (not facing out the door)
- ○ Use the front door regularly

- ○ Garbage
- ○ Old mail
- ○ Storage of rarely used belongings
- ○ Reminders of bad times
- ○ Anything unwelcoming (toss the scary lions and gargoyles)
- ○ Anything that prohibits walking freely to the front door
- ○ Broken or poorly functioning door
- ○ Anything related to a career you don't want
- ○ A mirror that faces the door
- ○ Squares or flat objects
- ○ Orange, yellow or brown
- ○ Dead plants
- ○ Clutter, dirt, dust, messes

Yard

Represents the Quality of the Energy that Surrounds You
Allow it to be Natural, Friendly and Easy

Add, remove or improve as many of the items below as possible in your yard.

+

- Fountain, water or symbols of water near the front door
- Plants and trees native to the area
- Round outdoor table
- Things that move (e.g., flags, windsocks)
- Pots made of natural materials (e.g., ceramic, wood, metal)
- Curved pathways
- Good lighting
- Things to attract wildlife (e.g., bird baths, flowers for butterflies)
- Keep the space around doors open

−

- Visible garbage
- Plastic pots
- Straight pathways
- Narrow pathways
- Sharp-angled pathways
- Fake plants
- Dead plants
- Clutter, dirt, dust, messes

Tips to Improve Relationships with Your Neighbors!

- Put up wind chimes between your home and theirs (Make sure the noise won't annoy people.)

- Have pretty plants/flowers between your home and theirs

- Put up a flag between your home and theirs

- Add anything that feels colorful, pretty, cheerful, and distracting between your home and theirs

- Remove garbage and trash cans between your home and theirs

- Remove anything that feels negative or cold between your home and theirs

Closets, Drawers, Garage, Storage

Represents What You Hold On To - Many Times Unconsciously
Allow them to Feel Uncluttered, Open and Airy

Start with the closet or drawer you use the most. Add, remove or improve as many of the following items as possible. Then move on to the closet or drawer you use second most and so on.

+

- ○ Good lighting
- ○ Keep the door and drawers closed
- ○ Light colored walls
- ○ Only items you love dearly or use yearly (to the fullest extent possible)

−

- ○ Products no longer used
- ○ Anything that prohibits you from walking freely
- ○ Clothes no longer worn or liked
- ○ Anything broken, torn or with holes
- ○ Anything you don't feel good wearing
- ○ Clothes that no longer fit
- ○ Disorganization
- ○ Reminders of bad times, people or things
- ○ Overstuffed closets, drawers or storage areas
- ○ Clutter, dirt, dust, messes

How to Do Feng Shui by Goal in Any Room

How to Do Feng Shui by Goal in Any Room

Feng Shui supports nine areas of your life: Money, Fame & Reputation, Love & Marriage, Family, Health, Children & Creativity, Wisdom & Knowledge, Career and Helpful People & Travel. Each one of these areas is represented in every room in your house.

To attract good energy and outcomes in these different life areas follow the two easy steps.

Step One
Determine the life area you'd like to improve and go to that page in the book. Once you're on that page, you'll see how to find that specific life area in any room.

Step Two
After you identify the life area's location in the room,

add or remove as many of the items listed on the page as possible. If you have any questions about how to do this, please see the FAQs at the back of the book. Examples of different floor plans and where the different life areas exist in the room are on the last page of this book.

Where Each Feng Shui Life Area is in a Room

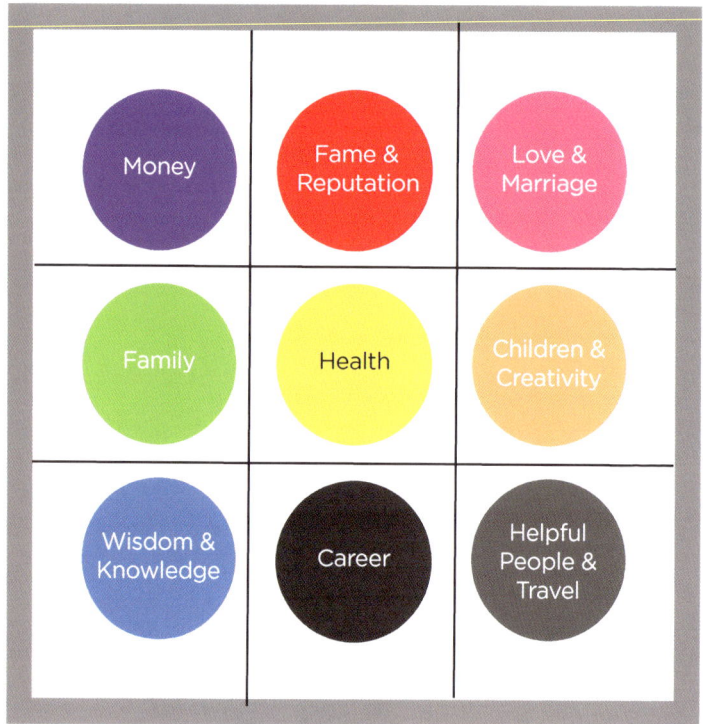

Money

Attract More Money to Your Life

Step 1

Stand in the doorway of the room you want to Feng Shui. Point to the farthest left corner. This corner is the Money area.

Step 2

Add or remove as many of the following items below as possible.

+

- ○ Round-leaf plants (ideally Jade plants)
- ○ Purple, red, gold and/or green
- ○ Moving objects or toys
- ○ Reminders of wealth
- ○ Mirror (not facing an exterior door)
- ○ Symbols of what you'll do with more money
- ○ Pictures, symbols or actual moving water
- ○ A container of spare change
- ○ Objects made from wood
- ○ Rectangular or free-form shapes

−

- ○ Trash cans
- ○ Anything broken or torn
- ○ Metal objects
- ○ Gray or white
- ○ Fire or symbols of it
- ○ Round objects
- ○ Triangular-shaped objects
- ○ Dead plants
- ○ Clutter, dirt, dust, messes

Fame & Reputation
Improve or Maintain Your Reputation

Step 1

Stand in the doorway of the room you want to Feng Shui. Mentally divide the far wall into three equal spaces. The middle area is the Reputation area.

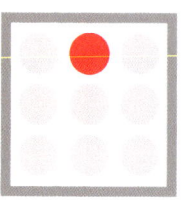

Step 2

Add or remove as many of the following items below as possible.

+

- ○ Red and/or green
- ○ Triangular, pointy, rectangular or columnar-shaped objects
- ○ Photos/symbols of people you admire
- ○ Upward things e.g., photos, of mountains, tall statues etc.
- ○ Stained glass
- ○ Symbols of fire
- ○ Lights
- ○ Photos/symbols of animals
- ○ Round leafed plants
- ○ Symbols of your achievements
- ○ Wood objects

−

- ○ Mirrors
- ○ Yellow, Orange, Brown, Blue and/or Black
- ○ Garbage
- ○ Tangled wires
- ○ Earth, water or symbols of them
- ○ Reminders of people you don't like
- ○ Symbols of who you don't want to be
- ○ Dead plants
- ○ Clutter, dirt, dust, messes

Love & Marriage

Attract Love or Improve Your Love Life and Marriage

Step 1

Stand in the doorway of the room you want to Feng Shui. Point to the farthest right corner. This corner is the Love & Marriage area.

Step 2

Add or remove as many of the following items as possible.

+

- ○ Candles
- ○ Fresh flowers
- ○ Pink, red and/or purple
- ○ Symbols that represent love to you
- ○ Identical things in pairs of two
- ○ Things that remind you of your partner or the partner you want to attract
- ○ Pictures of couples you admire and love
- ○ Objects made from earth
- ○ Square, pointy or columnar-shaped objects

−

- ○ Games
- ○ Anything work or fitness related
- ○ Storage
- ○ Things that feel or are cold
- ○ Anything broken or torn
- ○ Memories from old relationships or bad times
- ○ Anything that feels solitary (e.g., one candle)
- ○ Anything that feels negative
- ○ Metal, wood or symbols of them
- ○ Gray, white and/or green (not incl. flowers)
- ○ Dead plants
- ○ Clutter, dirt, dust, messes

Love & Marriage Tips!

- If you feel like there's something interfering with your current or potential relationship (or if you don't want anything to interfere with your relationship), make sure you have objects arranged in twos, not threes, around your home.

- In my experience, after implementing Feng Shui techniques to find love it takes between six and 12 months to find it. With that said, when you've Feng Shui'd your home for love, go live it up! Do everything you've wanted to do that could be more challenging when you have a partner - travel where you want, decorate your home how you want, hang out with who you want, spend the holidays how you want. Enjoy! Enjoy!

Family

Attract Good Energy Around Your Family

Step 1

Stand in the doorway of the room you want to Feng Shui. Look at the left side of the room. Mentally divide this area into three equal spaces. The middle area is the Family area.

Step 2

Add or remove as many of the following items as possible.

+

- Wood objects
- Green, blue and/or black
- Round-leaf plants
- Water or symbols of it
- Photos of family or families you admire
- Family heirlooms or gifts from family/Friends
- Free form, rectangular, vertical or column-shaped objects
- Identical objects in the same quantity as people you have or want to have in your family

−

- Metal objects and objects symbolic of fire
- Red, white and/or gray
- Round and/or triangular-shaped objects
- Anything broken or torn
- Dead plants
- Clutter, dirt, dust, messes

Tips to Improve Family Relationships!

Place pictures or mementos of happy memories with the family member(s) you struggle with in the Family area. Note: Nothing in Feng Shui has to be out in the open or visible. Feel free to hide these items behind a piece of furniture, art or in a drawer.

Health
Attract Good Health

Step 1

Stand in the doorway of the room you want to Feng Shui. Identify the exact center of the room. This center area is the Health area.

Step 2

Add or remove as many of the items below as possible.

+

- ○ Fire, sun or star symbols
- ○ Things that make you laugh or smile
- ○ Yellow, gold, orange and/or earth tones
- ○ Religious objects
- ○ Horizontal, square, triangular, pointy or flat objects
- ○ Items made from the earth (e.g., pottery, stones)

−

- ○ Wood objects
- ○ Gray, white and/or green
- ○ Columnar or rectangular-shaped objects
- ○ Anything medical no longer used/needed
- ○ Any reminders of unhealthy times
- ○ Dead plants
- ○ Clutter, dirt, dust, messes

Creativity & Children

Attract Creativity and Happy Children to Your Life

Step 1

Stand in the doorway of the room you want to Feng Shui. Look at the right most side of the room. Mentally divide this area into three equal sized squares. The middle area is the Children & Creativity area.

Step 2

Add or remove as many of the following items as possible.

+   −

- ○ Metal objects
- ○ White, gray, brown, yellow and/or orange
- ○ Round, square or flat objects
- ○ Candy, toys, games
- ○ TVs, music, lights, bells
- ○ Symbols or pictures of children
- ○ Symbols of creativity
- ○ Objects in the same quantity of children in your family or the number of children you would like in your family
- ○ Objects made from earth

- ○ Red, black and/or blue
- ○ Objects symbolic of fire or water
- ○ Triangular or pointy objects
- ○ Dead plants
- ○ Clutter, dirt, dust, messes

Wisdom & Knowledge

Attract More Wisdom and Knowledge

Step 1

Stand in the doorway of the room you want to Feng Shui. Mentally divide the wall where you're standing into three equal spaces. The left most area is the Wisdom & Knowledge corner.

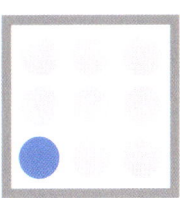

Step 2

Add or remove as many of the items below as possible.

+

- ○ Black, blue and/or earth tones
- ○ Books
- ○ Meditation items
- ○ Objects made from earth
- ○ Lights
- ○ Food
- ○ Water or symbols of it
- ○ Symbols/photos of smart or wise people
- ○ Symbols related to the skills or knowledge you want
- ○ Square or flat objects

−

- ○ Drugs or alcohol
- ○ Symbols of unwise ideas or people
- ○ Anything that distracts you from thinking clearly
- ○ Metal, wood, white, green and/or gray
- ○ Dead plants
- ○ Clutter, dirt, dust, messes

Career

Attract or Keep a Job You Love

Step 1

Stand in the doorway of the room you want to Feng Shui. Mentally divide the wall where you're standing into three equal spaces. The middle area is the Career area.

Step 2

Add or remove as many of the following items as possible.

+

- ○ Water or symbols of it
- ○ Black, blue white and/or gray
- ○ Welcoming sculptures, art or symbols
- ○ Flowers or plants
- ○ Free-form or round shapes
- ○ Mirrors (not facing an exterior door)
- ○ Glass
- ○ Metal objects
- ○ Symbols related to the career you want (e.g., related books, business cards of people who can help you or with positions you want, job descriptions, etc.

−

- ○ Squares or flat objects
- ○ Rarely used storage items or garbage
- ○ Objects made from earth
- ○ Reminders of bad times
- ○ Anything broken or torn
- ○ Anything that feels unwelcoming
- ○ Reminders of a career you don't want
- ○ Orange, gold, yellow
- ○ Dead plants
- ○ Clutter, dirt, dust, messes

Helpful People & Travel
Attract Helpful People & More Travel

Step 1

Stand in the doorway of the room you want to Feng Shui. Mentally divide the wall where you're standing into three equal spaces. The right most area is the Helpful People & Travel corner.

Step 2

Add or remove as many of the following items as possible.

- Bells
- Metal, gray, white and/or round objects
- Silver container with three wishes in it (see the next page for more info)
- Gray and/or white
- Religious objects or guardian angels
- Symbols of helpful people
- Symbols from your favorite places or places you want to travel

- Open drains
- Trash cans
- Torn or broken objects
- Reminders of bad or trying times
- Water, fire or symbols of them
- Red, blue and/or black
- Dead plants
- Clutter, dirt, dust, messes

How to Make Your Wishes Come True !

Write a wish on a piece of paper. Write it as if it has already been granted. For example, "I'm thrilled to have a job that's fulfilling and pays well" or "I feel fabulous since I met my weight loss goal". Make it as specific and focused as possible.

Write as many wishes as your would like. Place your them in a closed, silver container in the Helpful People & Travel area of the room you use the most. (The container doesn't need to be fancy. I've made them out of tin foil in the past.) Remove the wish once it's granted and replace it with another wish if you'd like!

If you have specific wishes for your work life, love life etc., feel free to put a container of work wishes on your desk or in your office (in the Helpful People & Travel corner). Similarly, you can put your love wishes in the Helpful People & Travel corner of your bedroom.

BONUS TIP: Add in photos or images of people and/or things you want in your life into your box!

The "Why" Behind What You Add, Remove and Improve

BEDROOM: Why You Add These Things

Solid Headboard To help you feel protected while you sleep.

Wall at the Head of the Bed Just like a headboard, this keeps you feeling safe while asleep. A wall at the head of your bed is more important than a headboard but having both are best.

Identical Nightstands and Lamps Because you want a relationship that's equal make both sides of the bed equal.

Comfortable Mattress and Comfy Sheets The comfier your mattress and sheets, the better you'll sleep (and the more in the mood for love all willl be).

Ability to See the Door While You Lay in Bed Sleeping well has much to do with feeling safe, and feeling safe has a lot to do with being able to see anyone who enters your door.

Art/Symbols of Love and Intimacy To reinforce the ideas of love and passion.

Ability to Easily Approach the Bed from Either Side You want a relationship that is equal, so make both sides of the bed equally accessible.

Dimmer on Lights To set the mood as you'd like, when you'd like.

Symbols of the Person You'd Like to Meet or Photos of You and Your Partner To support the energy of what you want or to keep the good energy around what you already have.

Red and/or Pink Accents Because these are the colors of love.

Candles and Good Scents To add romantic and sensual touches.

Any Identical Objects in Pairs of Two To promote the idea of both partnership and equality in that partnership. For example, two candles, two identical picture frames with both of you in them, two of the same/similar pieces of art, etc.

Close Bedroom and Closet Doors and Drawers at Night To keep any and all external energy - out.

BEDROOM: Why You Remove These Things

Using Someone Else's Mattress You want to attract only the energy you want.

You also want to keep anyone else's energy (especially bad energy) away from you.

Electronics, TVs, Computers, Books, Paperwork, Bills, Work or Fitness Equipment
These are distractions that often hold a lot of energy that could interfere with love and sleep.

Photos or Symbols of Anyone or Anything (including Religious Figures) Except You and Your Partner Because the bedroom is for you and your partner - ONLY. If you have kiddos, put your pictures of them in your Family area and/or Living Room.

Dirty Laundry It's probably pretty obvious how this literally and metaphorically could interfere with love and sleep, no?

Twin Bed This is a singular object and as such, a symbolic no-no in attracting and keeping love around.

Too Much White Because it feels cold and you want to attract warmth and the feeling of romance.

Mirror Facing the Bed A mirror doubles the size of everything. Bedrooms ideally feel small and cozy. Mirrors can prevent this sentiment. Mirrors also symbolize water, and you don't want your passion or your sleep to be "doused".

Storage Under the Bed or Anything Hanging Above Your Head Having stuff under your bed doesn't allow for energy to flow freely near the bed. It also clogs positive energy around love and sleep.
Anything above your head could fall on you while you sleep, and metaphorically you don't want anything "hanging over you" eight or more hours a day.

Water or Symbols of It Because water "douses" passion and the fire of love.

Bed Up Against a Window Because it can make you feel like someone or something can come up behind you. It can also hurt your ability to have a good night's sleep.

Reminders of Old Relationships, Bad Times or Anything Negative You spend a one-third of your life in your bedroom, you don't want to spend one-third of your life surrounded by bad memories, negative feelings and/or relationships that no longer exist.

Reminders of Why It's Hard to Sleep If you struggle with sleep the last thing you need is to be around reminders of things that keep you up at night.

Clutter, Dirt, Dust, Messes, Dead Plants They are one of the biggest Feng Shui no-no's. They prevent the flow of good energy and generally dampen the mood and overall feeling of any room, space or home.

LIVING ROOM: Why You Add These Things

Sofa Against a Wall While we don't often consciously think about it, we feel more relaxed and comfortable when our back is against a wall.

Place the Sofa So You Can Clearly See the Door While Seated Relaxing and having fun has much to do with feeling safe, and feeling safe has a lot to do with being able to see anyone who enters your door. (This probably dates back to living in caves and needing to know ASAP if a wooly mammoth or similar has come looking for dinner.)

Open Windows, Curtains and Blinds Regularly To let fresh air, light and new energy in and let old and stagnant energy out.

Symbols, Objects and Reminders of the Things You Want to Do and Want to Do More Of Because the Living Room is the area to celebrate what you love to do.

Photos of Happy Times and People You Enjoy To attract good social energy and to keep the good social energy you already have, keep images of what and who you enjoy.

LIVING ROOM: Why You Remove These Things

Furniture Against a Window Not having a solid back when you sit makes you feel vulnerable and as such uncomfortable.

Any Reminders of Bad Times These items shouldn't be anywhere in your house and especially not in the area designated for enjoyment in the present moment.

Anything that Reminds You of People You Don't Want To Spend Time With Because the Living Room is where you celebrate what you want to do and who you want to do it with.

Dead Plants Dead plants = dead energy.

Clutter, Dirt, Dust, Messes Clutter, dirt, dust and messes are Feng Shui no-no's. They prevent the flow of good energy and generally dampen the mood and overall feeling of any room, space or home.

KITCHEN: Why You Add These Things

Immaculate Stove and Oven The Kitchen is the heart of the home, and the stove is the heart of the Kitchen. The stove is one of the most important belongings in the home. Keep it clean to support a clean bill of health. (Side note: Anytime I feel a cold coming on, I triple check the stove to make sure it's extra sparkly clean.)

Only Keep Things on the Counter You Use Daily The Kitchen is symbolic of your health and you very likely don't want your health to be clogged and cluttered. As such, your kitchen shouldn't be clogged and cluttered either.

Symbols and Reminders of What Health Looks Like to You To reinforce the idea that where you eat and what you eat should be healthy.

Good Lighting Light is positive energy. As the Kitchen is the focal point of health, ensure it's well lit.

Yellow It's the color for health in Feng Shui.

A Bowl of Fruit on Your Table An overflowing bowl of fruit symbolizes an overflowing abundance of health and bonus (!) wealth.

Round-Leaf Plants They're symbolic of soft, constantly growing and living energy. Also note that, pointed-leaf plants are typically symbolic of harsh, cutting energy.

KITCHEN: Why You Remove These Things

Visible Knives Knives feel threatening, and you don't want your health to feel endangered.

Leaky Faucets They symbolize losing your health, and also, your wealth.

Dirty Dishes Not taking care of your dishes is symbolic of not taking care of your health.

Chipped or Broken Dishes They symbolize broken or damaged health.

Broken Appliances Broken appliances (or broken anything) symbolize broken health in the Kitchen.

Unused or Significantly Damaged Pots/Pans Because you don't want damaged goods associated with your health. (Also, damaged pots and pans seem a bit un-sanitary to cook on, no?)

Anything that Feels Unhappy or Unhealthy Because an important part of a healthy lifestyle is a positive outlook and a healthy feeling environment.

Food 12+ Months Old that You'll Never Eat There is nothing about old and unused food that feels healthy.

Dead Plants Dead plants = dead energy.

Clutter, Dirt, Dust, Messes Clutter, dirt, dust and messes are some of Feng Shui biggest no-no's. They prevent the flow of good energy and generally dampen the mood and overall feeling of any room, space or home.

BATHROOM: Why You Add These Things

Good Lighting Good light is good energy.

Good Ventilation Because wellness and vitality includes fresh and clean air.

Keep Toilet Seats Down To keep energy, health and wealth from escaping

Keep Drains Closed To keep energy from escaping.

Symbols, Objects and Reminders of What Vitality Looks Like To keep wellness and vitality in the front of your mind.

Round-Leafed Plants They're symbolic of soft, constantly growing and living energy. Also note, pointed-leaf plants are typically symbolic of harsh, cutting energy.

Open Windows, Curtains and Blinds Regularly To let fresh air, light and new energy in and let old and stagnant energy out.

Photos or Symbols of Nature To provide the feeling of health, growth and natural beauty.

BATHROOM: Why You Remove These Things

Expired Toiletries Because they're, literally, unhealthy (not to mention clutter).

Expired or No Longer Used Medicine Because they're reminders of unhealthy, or less healthy, times.

Clogged Drains They're symbolic of blocked energy.

Anything Broken or Torn Because broken and torn objects in the bathroom symbolize broken and damaged vitality and wellness.

Dead Plants Dead plants = dead energy.

Clutter, Dirt, Dust, Messes Clutter, dirt, dust and messes are one of the biggest Feng Shui no-no's. They prevent the flow of good energy and generally dampen the mood and overall feeling of any room, space or home.

DINING ROOM: Why You Add These Things

Table that Fits Comfortably in the Room So energy and people don't feel cramped or stifled and so your health and wealth don't either.

Oval or Round Table So everyone feels equal regardless of where they sit.

An Even Number of Chairs To support balanced energy.

Bowl of Fruit in the Middle of the Table It represents an abundance of wealth and health.

Round-Leaf Plants Near the Table Plants are alive and growing energy - two sentiments that are great to have in any area of a home. Further, plants such as cacti and more pointed leaf plants typically give the feeling of unwelcoming, "prickly" energy, while round leafed plants feel gentle and cozy.

Reminders of Happiness and Abundance To remind you that you've had these before and can easily have them again.

Dimmer on Lights To allow for soothing or bright energy - depending on what you desire.

Photos / Symbols of Wealth and Health To reinforce the symbolism (holding onto health and wealth) of the Dining Room.

Mirror That Reflects What's On the Table To double the appearance of health and wealth.

If You Have an Open Floor Plan, Have a Visual Break to Delineate the Dining Room To give the area that is symbolizes and celebrates of maintaining health and wealth its own special space.

Open Windows, Curtains and Blinds Regularly To let fresh air, light and new energy in and let old and stagnant energy out.

DINING ROOM: Why You Remove These Things

Clocks They encourage people to rush.

Electronics, TVs, Computers They're distractions and you don't want to distract the energy that's helping you hold onto health and wealth.

Chipped or Broken Dishes Damaged dishes = damaged health and/or wealth.

Seats Against Windows or With Backs to the Door
When people can't see if someone or something going to come up behind them, it makes them feel vulnerable and uncomfortable. Note: Seats against a window is less of a no-no if your dining room isn't on the first floor of your home or building.

Glass Dining Tables They're thought to create overly cautious and uncomfortable energy.

Dead Plants Dead plants = dead energy.

Clutter, Dirt, Dust, Messes Clutter, dirt, dust and messes are one of the biggest Feng Shui no-no's. They prevent the flow of good energy and generally dampen the mood and overall feeling of any room, space or home.

OFFICE/CUBE: Why You Add These Things

Arrange Your Desk So Your Back is Against a Wall Arrange your desk to clearly see the door while seated. The fear that someone could sneak up behind you is something our caveman and woman brains have yet to evolve out of. As such, it can create uneasiness, a less than ideal work environment and even more difficult energy to overcome to be successful. Also note, that having your back against a window is okay as long as you're not on the first floor. P.S. If you can't move your desk so that you face the door, put a mirror up so you can see behind you.

Arrange Your Desk So You Can Clearly See the Door While Seated To eliminate the feeling that someone can sneak up behind you.

Inspirational Images or Symbols To keep the energy around you about striving and succeeding.

Reminders of Where You Want Your Career to Go and What Your Success Will Look Like To surround yourself with ideas of where you're headed. For example, if you're trying to get into a particular business school, put a brochure from that business school in this area.

If you're trying to get a new job, print out your email correspondence with them or a business card you've received and put it in this area.

Round-Leaf Plants Plants are alive and growing energy - two sentiments that are great to have in any area. Further, plants such as cacti and more pointed-leaf plants typically give the feeling of unwelcoming, "prickly" energy, whereas round-leaf plants feel gentle and cozy.

Successful Feeling Furniture and Decor To surround yourself with the feeling of success.

Jade Plants The jade plant is considered lucky and thought to attract wealth.

Any Positive Stress Reliever The best success is the lowest stress success. Therefore, put things in your office that help you take a load off.

Inspirational Quotes To feel empowered, surround yourself with things and ideas that feel empowering.

OFFICE/CUBE: Why You Remove These Things

Tangled Cords Tangled cords = tangled confused energy.

Files on Your Computer You No Longer Need
Because: Clutter.
Paperwork You No Longer Need or Use Anything you

no longer use, even if it's just paper, is considered cluttered and as such - must go.

Symbols, Objects or Reminders Related to a Career You Don't Want You only want to focus on what you want. If you have any paperwork, images, symbols or reminders of a career you definitely don't want or currently have and are trying to get rid of - make sure you don't have these items in your office - or ideally anywhere in your house.

Reminders of Hard or Bad Times Bad times = bad energy.

Dead Plants Dead plants = dead energy.

Clutter, Dirt, Dust, Messes Clutter, dirt, dust and messes are one of the biggest Feng Shui no-no's. They prevent the flow of good energy and generally dampen the mood and overall feeling of any room, space or home.

FRONT DOOR: Why You Add These Things

A Clean and Very Welcoming Welcome Mat You want to say all good energy is welcome here.

A Fountain, Water or Symbols/Images of Water Water is the primary element associated with the Front Door.

Healthy Plants or Flowers Plants and flowers are happy, healthy and alive, and you want all of that kind of energy at the entrance of your home.

Symbols of the Career You Want or Want to Keep To attract the energy around what you want (and to remind yourself where you're headed). These symbols can include photos of you in your career or photos related to your ideal career, business cards of someone who has your career or who can help you get your ideal career, job descriptions of your dream job or anything else that reminds you of your ideal career when you look at it. Remember, nothing in Feng Shui needs to be seen to work.

A Wreath and/or Welcoming Decor You want to make sure you are welcoming that good career energy (and good energy in general) into your home.

Wind Chimes To bring attention to the Front Door as well as to avoid stagnant energy and enliven energy around the door.

Mirrors (Not Facing Out the Door) They are symbolic of water, the primary element of the Front Door. Important: Make sure the mirror doesn't face out the door.

Use the Front Door Regularly To keep new energy flowing into your home and into your career.

FRONT DOOR: Why You Remove These Things

Garbage Because you don't want "garbage" energy.

Old Mail Old mail, if not needed, is just old clutter - recycle it!

Storage of Rarely Used Belongings The Front Door to the home is considered the mouth to all energy in the home. It's the #1 indicator of how the rest of the energy in the home will feel. You don't want that energy to feel rarely used and/or bogged down by unnecessary or unneeded stuff.

Reminders of Bad Times Bad memories hanging around = bad energy hanging around.

Anything Unwelcoming (Toss the Scary Lions and Gargoyles) You want the energy associated with entering your home to feel happy, light and welcoming.

Anything that Prohibits Walking Freely to the Front Door The front door is the "mouth" of the home, this is where all energy enters the home. It can't enter your home freely, if your door doesn't open easily.

Broken or Poorly Functioning Door If the main entrance to your home determines the overall energy of your home, you don't want it to be "broken" or "poorly functioning".

Anything Related to a Career You Don't Want Let's put exactly zero energy toward what we don't want, okay?

A Mirror that Faces the Door It pushes all that good energy you just worked so hard for, right back out the door.

Square or Flat Objects Square and flat items are associated with the earth element and the earth element is the unsupportive element for the Front Door.

Orange, Yellow and/or Brown Orange, yellow and brown are the colors associated with earth, the unsupportive element for the Front Door.

Dead Plants Dead plants = dead energy

Clutter, Dirt, Dust, Messes Clutter, dirt, dust and messes are one of the biggest Feng Shui no-no's.

YARD: Why You Add These Things

A Fountain, Water or Symbol of Water Near the Front Door Water is the element associated with the Front Door.

Plants and Trees Native to the Area Native plants and trees will do better than any other flora you can plant. Thriving plants around your house means thriving energy surrounding your house-and you.

A Round Outdoor Table If you have an outdoor table, a round table is best, so everyone can sit in an "equal" position.

Things that Move (Flags, Windsocks) To prevent energy from stagnating and to keep energy moving.

Plants in Pots Made of Natural Materials (Ceramic, Wood, Metal) To celebrate, integrate and surround yourself with nature and the natural. P.S. Plastic - not natural.

Curved Pathways To slow the energy of the outside world before it comes into your home.

Good lighting Good lights = good energy.

Things to Attract Wildlife (Bird Baths, Flowers for Butterflies) You want alive, natural and growing energy around your home.

Keep the Space Around Doors Open To allow the energy and people to freely enter the house.

YARD: Why You Remove These Things

Visible Garbage Because the yard is symbolic of the energy that surrounds your house, and you don't want garbage energy around you.

Plastic Pots Because they're made from chemicals (that are killing nature) and as such don't enhance nature or support the natural.

Straight Pathways They allow the energy of the outside world to enter the home too quickly.

Narrow Pathways They're thought to constrict the energy that's entering the home.

Sharp-Angled Pathways Sharp angles don't allow for the energy to gently arrive at your front door.

Fake Plants Fake plants = fake energy.

Dead Plants Dead plants = dead energy.

Clutter, Dirt, Dust, Messes Clutter, dirt, dust and messes are one of the biggest Feng Shui no-no's.

CLOSETS/DRAWERS/GARAGE/STORAGE: Why You Add These Things

Good Lighting To ensure you're shining light on, and enlightenment towards, what you're keeping and holding on to.

Keep the Door and Drawers Closed To enforce organization and control over the things you hold onto.

Light Colored Walls To make what you hold on to feel light versus heavy.

Items You Love Dearly or Use Yearly Closets and storage spaces symbolize what you hold on to. Make sure everything you hold on to, literally and metaphorically, are things you love dearly and/or use yearly.

CLOSETS/DRAWERS/GARAGE/STORAGE: Why You Remove These Things

Products No Longer Used Because anything you no longer use - no matter where it is - is clutter and interferes with the positive energy flowing to what you want and deserve.

Anything that Prohibits You from Walking Freely If you get "stuck" walking through your things, your energy does too, which means you'll likely feel "stuck" in life as well.

Clothes No Longer Worn or Liked Because they're clutter, and they don't make you feel good when you look at them. Surround yourself (to the extent possible) with things that make you feel good when you see them.

Anything Broken, Torn or With Holes Because this reflects you holding onto things, ideas and people who are broken and not of use to you.

Anything You Don't Feel Good Wearing Because what's closest to you will have the most significant positive or negative impact on you, and it's harder to get much closer to you than your clothes. Make sure they have a good impact on you.

Clothes that No Longer Fit Anything not used is clutter. Clutter prevents energy from flowing freely. Clogged up energy trapped in your closets probably means "stuck" feeling energy in your life.

Disorganization Disorganized closets = disorganized energy = disorganized life.

Reminders of Bad Times, People or Things Holding onto bad times = holding on to bad energy.

Overstuffed Closets, Drawers or Storage Areas Because it suggests that you hold on to too much to the point that these things control you - instead of the other way around.

Clutter, Dirt, Dust, Messes Clutter, dirt, dust and messes are one of the biggest Feng Shui no-no's. They prevent the flow of good energy and generally dampen the mood and overall feeling of any room, space or home.

MONEY: Why You Add These Things

Round-Leaf Plants (Ideally Jade Plants) While plants such as cacti and more pointed-leaf plants typically give the feeling of unwelcoming, "prickly" energy, round-leaf plants feel gentle and cozy. The round leaves also symbolize coins.

Purple, Red, Gold and/or Green Purple is the color of royalty in China. Red is the most powerful color in Feng Shui. Green and gold are, of course, the traditional colors of - money, money, money!

Objects or Toys that Move To attract positive and easy movement of money towards you.

Reminders of Wealth To keep the spirit of money, and why you want it, alive.

Mirror (Not Facing an Exterior Door) Mirrors make the Money area look bigger, and you always want "bigger" money.

Symbols of What You'll Do with More Money To "tell" they energy and yourself what you want. (You can't get it, if you don't ask for it.)

Pictures, Symbols or Actual Moving Water Because you want money to flow into your life. Make sure the water isn't stagnant - you don't want your financial situation to slow down or hit a road block. Water is also a symbol of wealth in China and Feng Shui. Water is the supportive element of the Money corner.

A Container of Spare Change It's a symbol of money, well, because it is money. It's also symbolic of financial abundance. Always put change you can spare in it and try not to take any out. Taking it out is a symbol of "lack". You only want an energy of abundance around your money and everything else in your life. Other good things to put in your spare change container are partially or mostly used gift cards, money from other countries, jewelry that you no longer wear and Monopoly money or money from other games. Extra credit if the container is wood and/or purple, green, yellow or red.

Objects Made from Wood Wood is the primary element of the Money corner.

Rectangular or Free-Form Shapes Rectangles are the shapes associated with wood, the primary element of the Money corner. Free-form shape associated with water, the supportive element of the Money corner.

MONEY: Why You Remove These Things

Trash Cans Because you don't want to be metaphorically of throwing your money away.

Anything Broken or Torn No one wants damaged goods in their financial department.

Metal Objects Metal is an unsupportive element to the Money corner.

Gray, White or Red Red is the color of fire, the unsupportive element to the Money corner. White and gray are the colors of metal, also an unsupportive element of the Money corner.

Fire or Symbols of It Fire, like metal, is an unsupportive element in the Money corner.

Round Objects Round or circular-shapes are associated with metal, an unsupportive element to the Money corner.

Triangular-Shaped Objects Triangles are the shapes associated with fire, an unsupportive element to the Money corner.

Dead Plants Dead plants = dead energy.

Clutter, Dirt, Dust, Messes Clutter, dirt, dust and messes are one of the biggest Feng Shui no-no's. They prevent the flow of good energy and generally dampen the mood and overall feeling of any room, space or home.

FAME & REPUTATION: Why You Add These Things

Red and/or Green Red is the color of the Fame & Reputation area and of the element associated with the reputation area - fire. Green is the color of wood, the supportive element to the Reputation area.

Triangular, Pointy, Rectangular, Columnar-Shaped Objects You always want your reputation to be high and move upward. Triangles are also the primary shape of the Reputation area.

Photos/Symbols of People you Admire To reinforce the type of reputation you're looking to build and maintain.

Upward Things i.e. Photos of Mountains, Tall Statues Because you always want your reputation to be high and move upward.

Stained Glass Because it's symbolic of fire.

Symbols of Fire Fire is the primary element of the Reputation area.
Lights Good light is good energy. Get as much good

energy to your Reputation area as possible.

Photos/Symbols of Animals Because animals are thought to have a lot of fire energy.

Round-Leaf Plants While plants such as cacti and more pointed-leaf plants typically give the feeling of unwelcoming, "prickly" energy, round-leaf plants feel gentle and approachable - good things to have when you want a good reputation. Plants also symbolize living, growing and healthy things - great symbolism to have in your Reputation area.

Symbols of Your Achievements To remind you of why you're worthy of a great reputation.

Wood Objects Wood is the supportive element of the Reputation area.

FAME & REPUTATION: Why You Remove These Things

Mirrors They represent water and you don't want them to "douse" the fire of your reputation.

Yellow, Orange, Brown, Blue, and/or Black Earth and water are the unsupportive elements to the Reputation area. The colors associated with earth and water are orange, yellow, earth tones, blue and black.

Garbage Because you don't want a "trashy" reputation.
Tangled Wires They're confusing and messy two

things you don't want associated with your reputation (or your life).

Earth, Water or Symbols of Them Earth and water are the unsupportive elements of the Reputation area.

Reminders of People You Don't Like This area is all about who you are and who you want to be.

Symbols of Who You Don't Want to Be Because everything should only be about who you are and will be.

Dead Plants Dead plants = dead energy.

Clutter, Dirt, Dust, Messes Clutter, dirt, dust and messes are one of the biggest Feng Shui no-no's. They prevent the flow of good energy and generally dampen the mood and overall feeling of any room, space or home.

LOVE & MARRIAGE: Why You Add These Things

Candles To include symbols of love and romance.

Fresh Flowers Similar to candles, fresh flowers enhance the idea of love and romance.

Red, Pink and/or Purple Because these are the colors of love

Symbols that Represent Love to You To reinforce the idea of love and the love you're looking for.

Identical Things in Pairs of Two Such as candles, potted plants, pillows, picture frames, art work, sculptures. The idea is to support the concept of partnership and equality.

Things that Remind You of Your Partner or the Partner You Want to Attract If you know what you're looking for, it's easier to find it. And if you honor what you have, it's easier to keep it.

Pictures of Couples You Admire and Love There's no better symbol of love - than actual love. Put pictures of couples you honor in your Love & Marriage corner (just don't put pictures of other people in your bedroom).

Objects Made from Earth Because earth is the primary element of the Love corner.

Square, Pointy or Columnar-Shaped Objects Square is the shape of earth, the primary element of the Love corner. Columnar and pointy objects are the shape associated with Fire, the supportive element of the Love & Marriage corner.

LOVE & MARRIAGE: Why You Remove These Things

Games We're just done with those in our relationships—put the games in your Children & Creativity area instead.

Anything Work or Fitness Related Exercise equipment, papers, books and electronics are all big distractions—you want to be focused on each other.

Storage You don't want a relationship with baggage.

Things that Feel or Are Cold Who wants cold love?

Anything Broken or Torn No one wants damaged goods in their love department.

Memories from Old Relationships or Bad Times In order to be in the new, you need to get out of the old.

Anything that Feels Solitary (e.g., One Candle) You want to be in a twosome not an alone-some. To avoid solitude, always put things in pairs of two. Extra credit for identical objects, as you want to attract a relationship that's equal. Avoid things in threes to prevent an outside influence or person from impacting your relationship.

Anything that Feels Negative We're all done with that in our relationships.

Metal, Wood or Symbols of Them Metal and wood are the unsupportive elements to earth, the primary element of the Love corner.

Gray, White and/or Green Gray and white are the colors associated with metal. Green is the color associated with wood. Metal and wood are the unsupportive elements to the Love corner.

Dead Plants Dead plants = dead energy.

Clutter, Dirt, Dust, Messes Clutter, dirt, dust and messes are one of the biggest Feng Shui no-no's. They prevent the flow of good energy and generally dampen the mood and overall feeling of any room, space or home.

FAMILY: Why You Add These Things

Wood Objects Wood is the primary element of the Family area.

Green, Blue and/or Black Green is the color of wood (the primary element associated with the Family area). Blue and black are the colors associated with water, the supportive element in the Family area.

Round-Leaf Plants While plants such as cacti and more pointed leaf plants typically give the feeling of unwelcoming, "prickly" energy, round-leaf plants feel gentle and cozy.

Water or Symbols of It Water is the supportive element to wood, the primary element associated with the Family area.

Photos of Family or Families You Admire To help attract good and positive "family" energy and to reinforce the ideas of love and family longevity.

Family Heirlooms or Gifts from Family/Friends To celebrate family.

Free Form, Rectangular, Vertical or Columnar-Shaped Objects Vertical, rectangle and columns are the shapes associated with wood, the primary element of the Family area. Free-form objects are symbolic of water, the supportive element to the Family area.

Identical Objects in the Same Quantity as People You Have, or Would Want to Have in Your Family To help support the idea of togetherness, cohesiveness and collectiveness of family.

FAMILY: Why You Remove These Things

Metal Objects and Objects Symbolic of Fire Because they're the unsupportive elements to the Family area.

Red, White and/or Gray Because these are the colors associated with fire and metal, the unsupportive elements in the Family area.

Round and/or Triangle-Shaped Objects Round shapes are associated with metal, and triangles are associated with fire. Metal and fire are the unsupportive elements to the Family area.

Anything Broken or Torn Broken or torn objects are symbolic of broken or torn relationships.

Dead Plants Dead plants = dead energy.

Clutter, Dirt, Dust, Messes Clutter, dirt, dust and messes are one of the biggest Feng Shui no-no's.

HEALTH: Why You Add These Things

Fire, Sun or Star Symbols Fire is the supportive element to earth, and earth is the element associated with the Health area. The sun, stars and fire (of course) are symbols of fire.

Things that Make You Laugh or Smile Because laughter is the best medicine.

Yellow, Gold, Orange and/or Earth Tones These are the colors associated with earth, the primary element of the Health area.

Religious Objects So others look over your health - the most important thing to look after.

Square, Flat, Triangular or Pointed Objects Horizontal and square are are associated with earth, and earth is the element of Health. Fire is the supportive element of earth, and pointed objects are the shape associated with fire.

Items Made from Earth Materials (e.g., Pottery, Stones) Earth is the primary element of Health.

HEALTH: Why You Remove These Things

Wood Objects Wood and metal are the unsupportive elements to the Health area. Columnar and rectangular objects are associated with wood and metal.

Gray, White and/or Green Green, gray and white are the colors associated with metal and wood, the unsupportive elements to the Health area.

Columnar or Rectangular-Shaped Objects Wood is the unsupportive element in the Health area. Columnar and rectangular shapes are associated with wood.

Anything Medical No Longer Used or Needed To remove the idea of previous poor health and to avoid hanging onto the identity and memories of less healthy times.

Any Reminders of Unhealthy Times Let yourself be surrounded with only healthy ideas and memories.

Dead Plants Dead plants = dead energy.

Clutter, Dirt, Dust, Messes Clutter, dirt, dust and messes are one of the biggest Feng Shui no-no's. They prevent the flow of good energy and generally dampen the mood and overall feeling of any room, space or home.

CREATIVITY & CHILDREN: Why You Add These Things

Metal Objects Metal is the primary element associated with the Children & Creativity area.

White, Gray, Brown, Yellow and/or Orange White and gray are the colors associated with metal, the primary element of the Children & Creativity area. Yellows, browns and oranges are the colors of earth, the supportive element of the Children & Creativity area.

Round, Square or Flat Objects Metal is the primary element of the Children & Creativity area, and round shapes are associated with metal. The supportive element to the Children & Creativity area is earth, and the shape associated with earth is square (or flat objects).

Candy, Toys, Games Because they symbolize play, youthful energy, and fun.

TVs, Music, Lights, Bells They, like children and creativity, are energetic.

Symbols or Pictures of Children To attract children to you and keep the energy of children around you (if this is something you want, of course).

Symbols of Creativity To attract and keep creativity near you.

Objects in the Same Quantity of Children in Your Family or the Number of Children You Want to Have in Your Family To enforce the idea of your family as a whole or to attract the family you desire.

Objects Made from Earth Earth is the supportive element to the Children & Creativity area.

CHILDREN & CREATIVITY: Why You Remove These Things

Red, Black and/or Blue Red is the color associated with fire, and black and blue are the colors associated with water. Fire and water are the unsupportive elements in the Children & Creativity area.

Objects Symbolic of Fire or Water Fire and water are the unsupportive elements to the Children & Creativity area.

Triangular or Pointy Objects Triangular and pointed shapes are associated with fire, the unsupportive element to the Children & Creativity area.

Dead Plants Dead plants = dead energy.

Clutter, Dirt, Dust, Messes Clutter, dirt, dust and messes are one of the biggest Feng Shui no-no's. They prevent the flow of good energy and generally dampen the mood and overall feeling of any room, space or home.

WISDOM & KNOWLEDGE: Why You Add These Things

Black, Blue and/or Green These are the colors associated with the Wisdom & Knowledge area.

Books Because they're full of knowledge (usually).

Meditation Items To keep your mind clear, pure, open and without, ahem, clutter.

Objects Made from Earth Earth is the primary element of the Wisdom & Knowledge area.

Lights Good lighting is important everywhere in Feng Shui. Lights help illuminate knowledge and allow you to see the pathway to new skills.

Food Because a fed body helps to feed your mind.

Water or Symbols of It Water is the supportive element to the Wisdom & Knowledge area.

Symbols/Photos of Smart or Wise People To inspire wisdom and knowledge.

Symbols Related to the Skills or Knowledge You Want To attract "smart" energy.

Square or Flat Objects The square is the shape associated with earth, and the primary element associated with the Wisdom & Knowledge area.

WISDOM & KNOWLEDGE: Why You Remove These Things

Drugs or Alcohol Because they certainly don't make you smarter.

Symbols of Unwise Ideas or People Why this isn't a good idea is obvious, right?

Anything that Distracts You From Thinking Clearly To make sure you're always on your intellectual toes.

Metal and Wood, White, Gray and/or Green Metal and wood are the unsupportive elements to the Wisdom & Knowledge area. White, gray and green are the colors associated with metal and wood.

Dead Plants Dead plants = dead energy.

Clutter, Dirt, Dust, Messes Clutter, dirt, dust and messes are one of the biggest Feng Shui no-no's. They prevent the flow of good energy and generally dampen the mood and overall feeling of any room, space or home.

CAREER: Why You Add These Things

Water or Symbols of It Because water is the primary element of the Career area.

Black, Blue, White and/or Gray Water is the primary element of the Career area. Black and blue are the colors associated with water. White and gray are the colors of metal - the supportive element to the Career area.

Welcoming Sculptures, Art, Symbols To welcome good energy into your Career area.

Flowers or Plants To symbolize life, growth and happiness in your Career area.

Free-Form or Round Shapes Free-form is the shape associated with water, the primary element of the Career area. Round is the shape of metal, the supportive element to the Career area.

Mirrors (Not Facing an Exterior Door) Mirrors and glass symbolize water, the primary element associated with the Career area.

Glass Glass is symbolic of water, the primary element to the Career area.

Metal Objects Metal is the supportive element to your Career area.

Symbols Related to the Career You Want To attract the exact energy you want related to your career. For example, you could add the business card of someone who can help you get a new role or the business card of someone who has a role similar to the one you want. You could also add job descriptions of a position you're applying for, photos, books and/or symbols of what you'd be doing at your ideal job or objects/words related to how you'd feel having your perfect career.

CAREER: Why You Remove These Things

Squares or Flat Objects Square and flat objects are the shapes associated with earth, the unsupportive element to the Career area.

Storage and Garbage Storage tends to be clutter, and you don't want any cluttered energy associated with your career. Also, crap in this area is crap in your career.

Objects Made From Earth Earth is considered the unsupportive element to the Career area.

Reminders of Bad Times These shouldn't be anywhere in your home, and especially not in your Career area, if you want to attract good energy to your profession.

Anything Broken or Torn Jobs are hard enough without attracting broken or worn out energy around them.

Anything that Feels Unwelcoming You want to welcome good career energy with open arms.

Reminders of a Career You Don't Want To get what you want, only have energy related to what you want around you.

Orange, Gold, Yellow These are the colors of earth, the unsupportive element to the Career area.

Dead Plants Dead plants = dead energy.

Clutter, Dirt, Dust, Messes Clutter, dirt, dust and messes are one of the biggest Feng Shui no-no's. They prevent the flow of good energy and generally dampen the mood and overall feeling of any room, space or home.

HELPFUL PEOPLE & TRAVEL: Why You Add These Things

Bells To stimulate energy in this area. Added bonus, they're typically metal - the element associated with the Helpful People & Travel corner.

Metal, Gray and White and/or Round Objects Metal is the element of the Helpful People & Travel corner. Gray and white are the colors associated with metal. Round is the shape related to metal.

Silver Container with Three Wishes In It To manifest your dreams into fruition.

Religious Objects or Guardian Angels To have helpful people from beyond support you.

Symbols of Helpful People To show gratitude for them and encourage more people like them to be around you.

Symbols from Your Favorite Places or Places You Want to Travel To show appreciation for the places you've been able to travel to and to send energy towards the places where you will be going next.

HELPFUL PEOPLE & TRAVEL: Why You Remove These Things

Open Drains Because your energy runs right out of them.

Trash Cans You want high quality people and travel in your life - not garbage.

Torn or Broken Objects Damaged objects = damaged energy.

Reminders of Bad or Trying Times The Helpful People & Travel corner, like all corners and areas, need to be all about good energy. Get rid of as many bad memories as you can.

Water, Fire or Symbols of Them Water and fire are the unsupportive elements of the Helpful People & Travel corner.

Red, Blue and/or Black Red, blue and black are the colors associated with fire and water, the unsupportive elements of the Helpful People & Travel corner.

Dead Plants Dead plants = dead energy.

Clutter, Dirt, Dust, Messes Clutter, dirt, dust and messes are one of the biggest Feng Shui no-no's. They prevent the flow of good energy and generally dampen the mood and overall feeling of any room, space or home.

FAQs and Examples of Room Layouts

Feng Shui FAQs

What if my room isn't a perfect square?
If your room isn't a perfect square and you can't divide it into all nine areas, divide the room into nine equal-sized spaces (to the best of your ability given the layout of the room). Feng Shui, as is life, isn't always perfect. See the last page of this book for examples of how to find the different areas in different shaped rooms.

I've heard that you're supposed to Feng Shui the entire house, not just the rooms. What's true?
Most people live in a house with a floor plan that makes finding the different areas very difficult which causes many people to give up. For this reason, I suggest starting with the room you use the most or the room you think needs the most attention. Rooms typically have a much easier floor plan and allow you to confidently and easily get started with Feng Shui.

Of course, if you'd like you can start with finding the different areas for your entire house. On the other hand, you can do the rooms first to get your feet wet and then move on to the entire house.

Feng Shui FAQs

What do I do after I've completed the life area for one room?
When you've completed Feng Shui for one life area in a room, if you want to continue to focus on that one area of your life, go to the room you use second most (and then third most, etc.) and Feng Shui it for that chosen life area.

If your goal is overall improvement to the room you chose, then continue to Feng Shui that room for one of the other eight life areas. Continue through as many life areas as you want for that room.

How do I do Feng Shui if my house has an open floor plan?
If you want to Feng Shui a space with an open floor plan you have two options. You can consider it one big room and Feng Shui it, as such or you can consider it multiple rooms (e.g., the kitchen, living room and dining room) and Feng Shui each room separately based on where you feel the "door" / entrance to those rooms is located.

Feng Shui FAQs

What if my room has more than one door or entrance?
If there's more than one door to a room, use the door the architect of the home would consider the room's main door. If the doors are of equal importance, select the door you use the most.

Do I need to Feng Shui every room in my house or every life area in a room?
Don't feel pressured to Feng Shui every life area in a room. Start with the area of your life you most want to improve, and then move on to what you want to improve second most and so on. Similarly, don't feel pressured to Feng Shui every room in your home. Start with the one you use the most, and move on from there (if you want).

What are the most important areas of a home?
The Kitchen, Bedroom and Front Door are the most important areas of your home in Feng Shui. The bedroom is the most important of all as this is where you spend the most time.

Feng Shui FAQs

Am I supposed to add or get rid of everything that's listed?
Nope. Just do the best you can and make sure your room feels and looks right to you as a result of the things you're adding and removing. Sometimes just a little goes a long way.

What if I really love something that is not good Feng Shui for the area it is in?
Often when we love something that isn't ideal for one area but we move it to an area better suited from a Feng Shui perspective - we love it even more.

Give it a try. If it doesn't feel right in the new place and you still prefer it in the old place keep it where you love it and just pay attention to how the energy for that particular area of your life is feeling. If you're not getting what you want consider moving that item for two to four weeks and see if there's a shift towards what you desire.

Feng Shui FAQs

What should I definitely get rid of or do?
To the extent possible and feasible, remove anything that brings up bad memories or feels negative. Limit the number of items that are or feel cold. Keep pathways (inside and outside of the house) clear. Let the fresh air come in. Open windows regularly and blinds/curtains daily. Try not to store anything on the back of doors. It blocks the flow of energy - and is just generally kind of annoying.

What kind of plants should I have?
Ideally, plants should be round-leafed and not droopy. Avoid cacti (unless they're native to your area), dead plants and fake plants and flowers. But certainly don't toss any live plants that don't meet the ideal description. Anything that's alive, healthy and growing is good energy. Just make sure, for example, if you have a droopy or prickly plant in your Love & Marriage area that you've added some of the positives for this area to counteract it.

Feng Shui FAQs

What should I do if some of the advice seems to conflict with other advice?
There will be times when the advice for a room in the house conflicts with the basic Feng Shui life area advice. For example, in your bedroom it's recommended you only have items in pairs of two. In contrast, if you're trying to attract fertility, having objects in the same number of people you'd like in your family is recommended. In these cases, let your intuition and what's most important guide you.

Does everything I add in a room or an area need to be seen?
Nothing in Feng Shui has to be out in the open or visible. Feel free to put these items behind a piece of furniture, art or in a drawer.

What if what I add or remove makes my room look weird?
It's most important that your house looks and feels good to you. You don't need to make every addition and removal for Feng Shui to work. Only add or remove what feels good. Sometimes just a few changes can go a long way. Add or remove what feels right and see if there's a shift. If there is, then perfect. If not, add or remove a bit more.

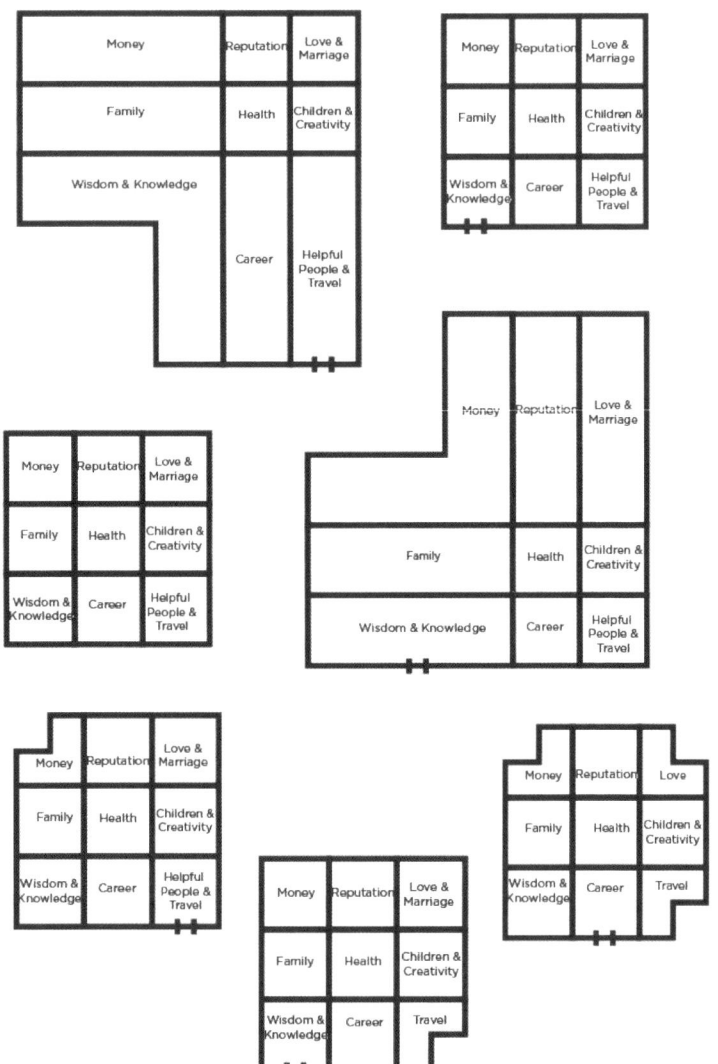

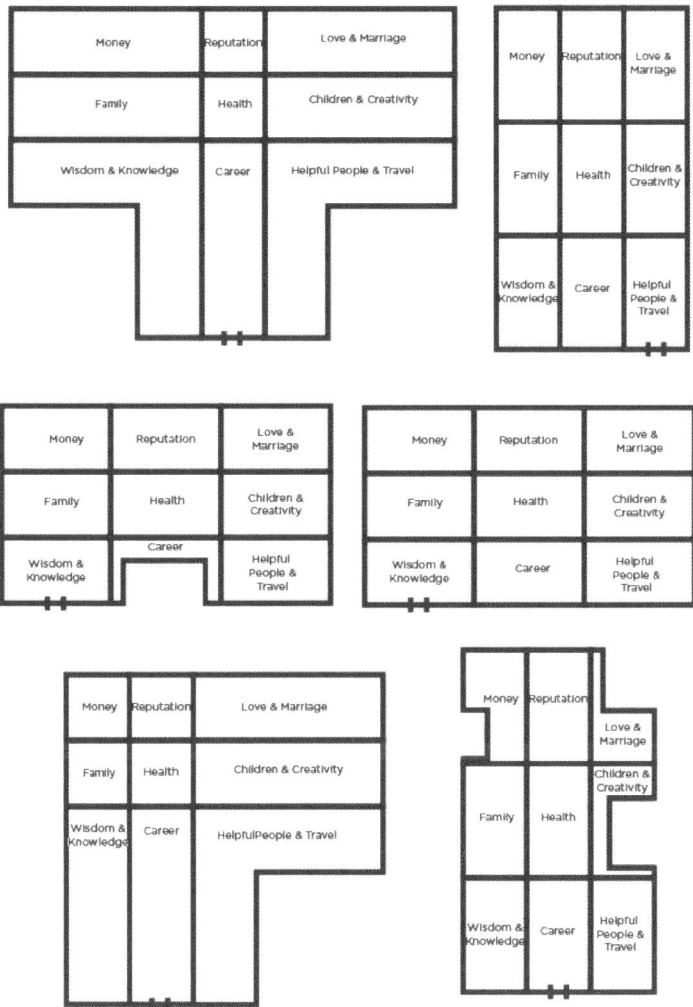

99

Contact Me

Questions, comments, feedback, consultation or class request?

linda@happyhousefengshui.com

Follow:
Facebook, Instagram Pinterest:
Happy House Feng Shui

Printed in Great Britain
by Amazon